TAYLOR'S HANDBOOK FOR THE INSTALLATION OF MASTER

The full ceremonies, including the Inner Working

(Excluding Investiture of Officers and Addresses)

First

Lewis Masonic

First edition first published 2005
Reprinted 2009, 2012, 2016, 2019
This impression 2022

ISBN 978 0 85318 249 8

Published by Lewis Masonic Ltd
166 Great North Road, Eaton Socon, St Neots, Cambs PE19 8EH

Printed in England.

Visit the Lewis Masonic website at www.lewismasonic.co.uk

CONTENTS

The Association for Taylor's Working

TAYLOR'S HANDBOOK FOR THE INSTALLATION OF MASTER

INTRODUCTION

Structure of the Book

In previous editions of Taylor's Ritual the Master, in order to install his successor, has been required to work from two separate books. Firstly, The Handbook of Craft Freemasonry (which includes the three degrees) is required for the presentation and obligation of the Master Elect and, after the Inner Working, for the salutations and presentations following his installation. Secondly, the Inner Working booklet is required to actually install him in the Chair.

To simplify matters the complete installation ceremony is now contained in this one book. The reader needs to refer to the main Handbook only for the addresses to the Master, Wardens and Brethren and for the Investiture of Officers.

The book is in four sections. The first contains general explanatory notes that give enhanced descriptions of actions and procedures in the other three sections. The second section contains the full installation ceremony, the third section is for the installation of a Past Master (induction), and the fourth is for a Master continuing in office for a second consecutive year (proclamation).

Aims of the Book

The ceremonial, other than the Inner Working, is reproduced from the main Handbook and requires little comment. On the other hand, compared with earlier editions, the Inner Working has been considerably enhanced with additional rubric and more detailed explanations of the signs.

From the many comments and queries received by the Association from users of the earlier editions of the Inner Working it was evident that these books contained several ambiguities and a number of vagaries. It was also wanting on information for the induction and proclamation ceremonial for Installed Masters.

In consequence, the watchwords adopted by the Committee in producing this new book have been **simplicity, clarity and completeness**. In particular, any new book must not only be easily followed by an experienced Past Master but also readily understood by a newly Installed Master.

The Guiding Principle

The Committee has deliberated for more than two years on the content of the Inner Working. This was followed by an open discussion with a representative cross-section of Past Masters of Lodges using Taylor's Working in order to gain feedback on its proposals.

In arriving at its conclusions the Committee has been guided by the principle that the Inner Working is not a Third Degree Lodge (as Master Masons are excluded), therefore the signs used should be those of an Installed Master and not those of the Third Degree.

For many lodges the new working may differ in certain respects from what they have practised previously – but it has always been understood within the Association that some lodges will wish to continue to practise their 'traditional' working. However, we hope that the logic behind the revised compilation will shine through and that lodges will indeed enjoy working from this new edition.

Acknowledgements

On behalf of the Association for Taylor's Working, I would like to express my thanks to the Chairman and members of the Executive Committee for the many hours of deliberation and discussion leading to the publication of this first edition of the Installation Handbook. I particularly thank Peter R Lewin PAGDC, Secretary of the Committee, who produced the many drafts and prepared the text for the publisher.

Michael F Bames PJGD, Life President.
May 2005.

THE ASSOCIATION FOR TAYLOR'S WORKING

The Association was formed on 30 November 1965 to act as a central body representative of Lodges and Lodges of Instruction practicising Taylor's Ritual. In addition it was to maintain a standard version of Taylor's Ritual, together with explanatory notes and rubric, to conform to well founded practice and principles, and to make such amendments as may, from time to time, be found necessary or expedient.

The Executive Committee forms a court of reference, capable of giving decisions on questions arising from the Rubric and of obtaining and providing advice and enlightenment on Masonic problems that may be referred to it.

The Association holds a Lodge of Improvement, under the sanction of Temple Lodge No. 101, devoted to teaching and demonstrating Taylor's Ritual. Committee meetings, followed by an LOI are held at Freemasons Hall, Great Queen Street, London WC2, commencing at 7.00pm.

Membership is open to all Lodges and Lodges of Instruction on the register of the United Grand Lodge of England and any Grand Lodge, recognised by the UGLE. Membership categories are for a representative of the Lodge or LOI or from any individual, provided they are Master Masons or above.

For further details of the Association; the cost of membership and the dates of Meetings, please contact the Secretary through Metropolitan Grand Lodge of London.

GENERAL NOTES

USE OF SN. OF F.

The D.C. on presenting the M.E. in the full installation gives the Sn of F. It is not considered appropriate to give the P. Sn. of the Third Degree which is used when in that Degree. (The Sn. of F. is also used when the S.W. presents the Cand. in the Second and Third Degrees.)

GRIP

The Grip of an I.M. as set out in the rubric indicates that it is only given by the I.M. and is not reciprocated.

TOKEN OF HUMILITY

There are several signs and tokens used in the Inner Working. The Token of Humility has been amply described when given by the I.M. It is suggested that it be used when the Brethren greet the new W.M. Alternatively the G.or R.Sn may be used.

THE V.S.L.

It is possible that some old, heavy and delicate Bibles may be damaged by closing it on the S. and Cs. It is therefore suggested that in such cases a suitable cloth may draped over the three G. Ls.

At the Induction of a Past Master, it is unnecessary for the M.E. to salute the V.S.L. after his re-affirmation as his previous Obligation is "binding upon him so long as he shall live".

SALUTING THE V.S.L.

The words *'with your lips'* when sealing the obligation on the V.S.L. has been removed as it is not lawful for some faiths to touch their S.L. The suggested wording used here is *'you will salute the V.S.L x times.'* Where appropriate for other faiths, the 'seal' will still be made *'with the lips.'*

MASTER CONTINUING IN OFFICE

This is the only proclamation and greeting. There are no perambulations and no presentation of the Working Tools. The Warrant, Book of Constitutions and Bylaws are not presented. The Investiture of Officers is normal.

If the address to the Master is to be delivered (optional), the first sentence should read:

"Worshipful Master, you having been proclaimed Master of this worthy and worshipful Lodge for a further year, cannot be insensible.........."

CEREMONY OF INSTALLATION
PART ONE

(The Lodge being open in the First Degree, the W.M. sounds his Gavel, one k., which is answered by S.W. and J.W.)

W.M. – W. Bro. *(surname only, who rises and gives Sp. and Sn. of First Degree)*, will you please occupy the S.W.'s chair. *(W.Bro. cuts Sn.) (D.C., squaring the Lodge, conducts the W.Bro. to r. of S.W. who removes his gauntlets and leaves them on top of the pedestal to await the newly invested S.W. Retaining his collar of office, S.W. vacates chair in favour of the W.Bro., who salutes W.M. in the First Degree and sits. D.C., squaring the Lodge, conducts the retiring S.W. to a seat in the NE and returns to his own seat.)*

W.M. – *(sounds his Gavel, one k., which is answered by S.W. and J.W.)* – W.Bro. *(surname only, who rises and gives Sp. and Sn. of First Degree)*, will you please occupy the J.W.'s chair. *(W.Bro. cuts Sn.)*

(D.C., squaring the Lodge, conducts the W.Bro. to r. of J.W. who removes his gauntlets and leaves them on top of the pedestal to await the newly invested J.W. Retaining his collar of office, J.W.

vacates chair in favour of the W.Bro. who salutes W.M. in the First Degree and sits. D.C., squaring the Lodge, conducts the retiring J.W. to a seat in the NE and returns to his own seat.)

W.M. – *(sounds his Gavel, one k., which is answered by S.W. and J.W.)* – W.Bro. *(surname only, who rises and gives Sp. and Sn. of First Degree)*, will you please act as I.G. *(W.Bro. cuts Sn.)*

(D.C., squaring the Lodge, conducts the W.Bro. to the I.G. Retaining his collar of office, I.G. vacates his seat in favour of the W.Bro., who salutes W.M. in the First Degree and sits. D.C., squaring the Lodge, conducts the retiring I.G. to a seat in the NE and returns to his own seat.)

W.M. – *(sounds his Gavel, one k., which is answered by S.W. and J.W.)* – Bro. Chaplain, Bro. Secretary, Bro.D.C., Bro.A.D.C. and Bro. Organist *(who all rise and give Sp. and Sn. of First Degree)*, will you please continue to act in your respective offices. *(the five officers cut Sn. and sit)*

W.M. – *(sounds his Gavel, one k., which is answered by S.W. and J.W.)* – Brethren, I now request the officers of my year to assemble in line along the N.

(The officers, squaring the Lodge where necessary, line-up under D.C.'s guidance along the N, and face S; the W.M. here usually addresses them with a general expression of thanks for their services during the year.)

W.M. – Will you now please file past so that I can thank you individually and will you then please return the collar with which I had the pleasure of investing you, to our Brother, the I.P.M., in passing.

(The officers turn left and, squaring the Lodge at NE corner, file past W.M. who rises, personally greets each officer in turn at l. of pedestal, and resumes his seat. Meanwhile, the I.P.M. has taken up a suitable position in SE. The officers, as they pass the I.P.M. remove their collars of office and hand them to him. Squaring the Lodge where necessary, the Chaplain, Secretary, D.C., A.D.C. and the Organist return to their usual places, while the remainder of the officers proceed to vacant seats in the Lodge. I.P.M. transfers collars to A.D.C. The Lodge is then opened in the Second Degree; D.C. attends to T.B. M.E., who is seated in the NE, removes his gloves and rises. D.C., squaring the Lodge, conducts the M.E. to a suitable position in mid-line of the Lodge, and stands to his r., both facing W.M.)

D.C. – *(gives Sp. and Sn. of Second Degree)*- W.M., I present to you Bro. *(full name)*, Master Elect of this Lodge to receive at your hands the benefit of Installation.

W.M. – Bro. D.C., your presentation shall be attended to, but I must first address a few observations to the Brethren, I shall then call the attention of Bro. *(surname only)* to those qualifications which are necessary in every Candidate for the Master's chair. *(D.C. cuts Sn. and squaring the Lodge, returns to his seat; M.E. remains standing facing W.M.)*

W.M. – *(sounds his Gavel, one k., which is answered by S.W. and J.W.)* – Brethren, from time immemorial it has been an established custom among Freemasons for each Lodge, once in every year at a stated period, to select from its Wardens and past Wardens a skilled Craftsman to preside over them in the capacity of Master. He must have been regularly balloted for and elected by the Master, Wardens, and Brethren in open Lodge assembled and be presented to a Board of Installed Masters to receive from a predecessor the benefit of Installation, the better to qualify him for the discharge of that important trust. Bro. *(surname only)*, you having been so elected and before you are presented to the Board, I claim your attention while I recite those qualifications which are essential in every Candidate for the Master's chair.

First: every Candidate for the office of Master must be of good report, true and trusty, and held in high estimation among his Brethren and Fellows. Secondly: he must have been regularly Initiated, Passed and Raised in the three established Degrees of the Order, be well skilled in the noble science, and have duly served the office of Warden in a regular Lodge. Thirdly: he should be exemplary in conduct, courteous in manner, easy of address, steady and firm in principle, well skilled in the Ancient Charges, Regulations, and Landmarks of the Order, able and willing to undertake the management of the work. Can you, my worthy Brother, accept the Mastership of this Lodge under these qualifications?

M.E. – *(gives Sp. and Sn. of Second Degree)*- I can, W.M. – *(cuts Sn.)*

W.M. – Then I claim your attention whilst our Bro. Secretary reads from the Book of Constitutions those Charges and Regulations to all of which your unqualified assent is necessary, which you will signify by the S. of F. after each clause, slightly bowing the head in token of submission.

(D.C., squaring the Lodge, conducts Secretary to the SE and returns to his own seat. Secretary gives Court Bow to W.M., turns to face M.E. and reads from the Book of Constitutions, the Ancient Charges and Regulations, numbered 1-15, pausing after each Charge for M.E. to signify. Secretary turns, gives Court Bow and, squaring the Lodge, is conducted to his seat by D.C. who then returns to his own seat.)

W.M. – Do you submit to and promise to support those Charges and Regulations as Masters have done in all ages?

M.E. – *(without Sp. or Sn.)* – I do.

W.M. – Then you will please step this way and take the S.O. of Master Elect. *(M.E. moves forward to W.M.'s pedestal.)*

W.M. – You will kneel as a F.C. (*or*, *You will be covered.) *(this having been done, M.E. places his r.h. on the V.S.L. and shows H.Sn. W.M. sounds his Gavel one k., which is answered by S.W. and J.W. All rise and, without taking Sp., come to order with the Sn. of F.)*

OBLIGATION

W.M. – *(to M.E.)* – Stating your names at length, repeat after me: I, *(M.E. states his full name)*, in the presence of T.G.G.O.T.U. and of this worthy and worshipful Lodge of F.C.Fs., regularly held, assembled and properly dedicated, do agree to accept the office of Master of this Lodge; and the duties of that high station, zealously, faithfully, and impartially to administer, to the best of my skill and ability, until the next period of election within the Lodge and until a successor shall have been duly elected and installed in my stead. I further solemnly promise that I will not, either during my Mastership, or at any time the Lodge may be under my direction, permit or suffer any

**Alternative wording should Cand. be Jewish*

deviation from the Ancient Customs and established Landmarks of the Order. I will not administer, nor suffer to be administered, any rite or ceremony contrary to, or subversive of, our Ancient Institution, but will maintain and uphold, pure and unsullied, the genuine principles and tenets of the Craft. I will observe, and to the utmost of my power enforce, a due obedience to those Charges and Regulations to which I have already given my assent, and in every respect conscientiously discharge my duties as a Ruler in the Craft and Master of this Lodge. So help me A.G. and keep me steadfast in this the S.O. of Master Elect.

(M.E. drops H. Sn.)

W.M. – As a pledge of fidelity and to render what you have repeated a S.O. you will salute the V. of the S.L.t. *(M.E. does so; all drop Sn. of F.; W.M. takes M.E.'s r.h. in his own)*. Rise, (*or*, *Be uncovered,) duly obligated, Master Elect.

(W.M. sits and Brethren resume their seats. D.C., squaring the Lodge, conducts M.E. to a seat in the SE and returns to his own seat. The Lodge is then opened in the Third Degree; D.C. attends to T.B.)

W.M. – *(sounds his Gavel one k., which is answered by S.W. and J.W.)* – Brethren, I must now request all below the rank of Installed Master, with

**Alternative wording should Cand. be Jewish*

the exception of the Master Elect, to retire from the Lodge.

(I.G. goes to the door, opens it, and retiring Brethren leave the Lodge without saluting: I.G. locks door and returns to his seat)

THE CEREMONY OF INNER WORKING NOW FOLLOWS. THE M. E. SHOULD BE MADE AWARE THAT THE I. P. M. WILL BE INVESTED DURING THIS PART OF THE CEREMONY.

INNER WORKING

(The Brethren below the rank of Installed Master with the exception of the M.E. having retired from the Lodge, the A.D.C., squaring the Lodge, places kneeling stool in the centre of the Lodge and returns to his seat. D.C., squaring the Lodge, conducts M.E. to kneeling stool and both stand facing E. I.M. sounds his gavel, one k., which is answered by S.W. and J.W.)

I.M. – Brethren, I declare this a duly constituted Board of Installed Masters.

D.C. – *(gives Sn. of F.*)* – W.M., I present to this Board of Installed Masters, Bro............. *(M.E.'s full name)*, duly obligated M.E., to receive from your hands the benefit of Installation.

I.M. – Bro. D.C., your presentation shall be attended to. *(D.C. drops Sn. of F. and returns to his seat: M.E. remains standing.)*

I.M. – *(sounds his Gavel, one k., which is answered by S.W. and J.W.)* Bro. – *(M.E.'s name)* – You will kneel on both knees. *(or,* – **You will be covered.) Brethren, let us pray. *(Brethren rise, turn*

**See General Note*

***Alternative wording should the Cand. be Jewish*

to face E., give Sn. of R. and may kneel on one k. on a convenient seat.)

Chaplain or I.M. – Vouchsafe Thine aid Almighty Father, Supreme Governor of the Universe, to our solemn rite and grant that this worthy and distinguished Brother, who is about to be numbered among the rulers in the Craft, may be endued with wisdom to comprehend, judgment to define, and ability to enforce obedience to Thy Divine laws. Sanctify him by Thy grace, strengthen him with Thy power, and enrich his mind with genuine knowledge, that he may be the better enabled to enlighten the minds of the Brethren and to consecrate this our mansion to the honour and glory of Thy Most Holy Name.

ALL – *(the following response may be chanted)* – So mote it be. *(all drop Sn. of R. Brethren resume standing position; M.E. rises, or, if Jewish, remains covered until after his obligation. A.D.C., squaring the Lodge, removes kneeling stool and returns to his place.)*

I.M. – *(to M.E.)* Bro.........*(Surname only)*, you have already taken an Obligation as regards your duties as Master of the Lodge. You will now take another Obligation as regards the secrets restricted to the Master's Chair. Please step this way *(M.E. moves forward to W.M.'s pedestal)*, kneel on both knees, (*or*, – **You will be covered.)

***Alternative wording should the Cand. be Jewish*

place both hands on the V. of the S.L. *(I.M. sounds his gavel, one k., which is answered by S.W. and J.W.; Brethren, without taking Sp., come to order with Sn. of F.)*

I.M. – Stating your names at length, repeat after me: I, *(M.E. states his full name)*, in the presence of T.M.H. and of this worthy and worshipful Board of Installed Masters, duly constituted, regularly assembled and properly dedicated, do hereby and hereon *(W.M. presses the fs. of b.hs. on those of the M.E., then lowers the ps. of his hs. on V.S.L.)*, most solemnly and sincerely swear *(W.M. resumes Sn. of F.)* that I will ever conceal and never divulge any or either of the secrets restricted to the Master's Chair to anyone in the world, unless it be to an Installed Master or to a Candidate duly elected to that office, and not even then, unless in the presence of two or more Installed Masters at a meeting duly convened for that purpose. These several points I solemnly swear to observe, without evasion, equivocation, or mental reservation of any kind. So help me T.M.H. and keep me inviolate in this, the S.O. of an Installed Master.

I.M. – As a pledge of fidelity and to render what you have repeated a S.O. binding upon you so long as you shall live, you will Salute the V.of the S.L. t.t. *(M.E. does so; all drop Sn. of F.; I.M. removes M.E.'s l.h. from the V. of the S.L. and then lifts and holds M.E.'s r. forearm* *with his l.h.).*

I.M. – The symbolic penalty which a M.E. was at one time called on to repeat in his Obligation, was that of having t.r.h.s. at the w. *(I.M. demonstrates "s. at the w.")* and t.o.t.l.s. *(I.M. places M.E.'s r.h. on M.E.'s l.s.)*, there left to w. and decay; and this is the P.Sn. of an I.M.

I.M. – Let me once more direct your attention to the three G.Ls. in Freemasonry, which are the V. of the S.L., the S. and the Cs. *(I.M. points to each in turn)*. The V. of the S.L. is that G.L. which will guide you to all truth, direct your steps in the paths of happiness and point out to you the whole duty of man. The S. teaches you to regulate your life and actions according to Masonic line and rule and to harmonise your conduct by the principles of morality and virtue. The Cs. remind you to limit your desires in every station of life, so that, rising to eminence by merit, you may live respected and die regretted. *(M.E. remains kneeling, (standing if Jewish) I.M lowers M.E.'s a., removes gauntlets, places them on pedestal and moves out of the pedestal to r. of M.E.)*

I.M. – Rise, *(I.M. assists M.E. to rise.)* *(or,** Be uncovered,) duly obligated, Installed Master. *(I.M. moves M.E. clockwise away from the pedestal and places him in the SE facing N; steps back three paces and stands facing him; all remain standing.)*

**Alternative wording should the Cand. be Jewish*

I.M. – Traditional history informs us that when the Temple at Jerusalem was completed by the wisdom of K.S., supported by the strength of K.H. and aided by the beautifying hand of H.A., the sovereigns of the surrounding nations sent ambassadors to congratulate K.S. on the completion of that stately and superb edifice, the regal splendour and unparalleled lustre of which were said to have surpassed imagination. The Queen of Sheba, to whom the fame of the King had reached, not content with sending an embassy, herself journeyed to Jerusalem attended by a numerous retinue laden with costly presents. On her arrival she was received by K.S. who accompanied her to view the Temple.

On entering the sacred edifice, the King, perceiving Adoniram at a distance, beckoned him t.t. thus *(I.M. demonstrates, by turning his head about half-way to the right, i.e. about 45°, and stretching out his r.a. in that direction, then touching his r.s. with the first two fingers of his r.h.; M.E. copies; I.M. repeats this beckoning sign twice more, again being copied each time by M.E.with his r.h)*. Adoniram, on approaching his Royal Master was about to kneel *(M.E., prompted by D.C., attempts to kneel on r.k.)*, which the King prevented by taking him thus *(I.M. steps forward and takes M.E. by the r. upper arm with his l.h. then gives the G. of an Installed M. by taking a grip on* *top of the r.forearm of the M.E. with his r.h*.)*.

I.M. –Rise ......, which signifies ...., or literally .... *(I.M. releases his l.h. and, emphasizing his grip on M.E.'s forearm with the r.h.)* – this is the G. of an Installed Master *(I.M. releases his r.h. and resumes his former position facing S.)*

When the royal party had completed their inspection and were about to retire, Adoniram, in token of humility, saluted the King t.t. thus *(I.M. demonstrates by touching his forehead with the fingertips of the r.h. at the same time bowing slightly from the waist, and by moving the r.f. backwards with a circular motion whilst sweeping the r.h. downwards and backwards as far as the r.k. This salute could be construed as being similar to a Cavalier doffing his hat.)* This is the Salutation of a Master of our Art and Science, otherwise known as the Token of Humility. *(I.M. resumes upright position and M.E. copies the salutation. I.M. repeats the salutation twice more, again copied each time by the M.E.)*.

I.M. – Hence are derived the Signs, G., and Word of an Installed Master, and the Salutation of a Master of our Art and Science. *(D.C. comes forward bearing Master's badge on a cushion and stands at l. of I.M. M.M.'s badge is removed from M.E.)*

**See General Note*

I.M. – I now invest you with the distinguishing badge of an Installed Master *(I.M. picks up badge, and places it in position.)*, and long may you live to wear it with credit to yourself and to the advantage of the Craft. I also invest you with the Master's Collar *(I.M. removes his Collar of Office and invests M.E. as W.M.)*, which is the highest honour the Lodge can confer on any of its members. To this Collar is attached the S. *(I.M. indicates the Jewel)*, an instrument which forms the rude and proves the perfect mass, and is justly applied by Installed Masters to inculcate the principles of piety and virtue. Masonically speaking it should be the guide of all your actions. *(D.C. returns to his place.)*

(I.M., with his r.h., grips the W.M. with the G. of an Installed Master, places on his own l.s. the l.h. of the W.M. and places his own l.h. on the l.s. of the W.M. Maintaining the relative positions of the a. and h., I.M. instructs the W.M. to step off with the l.f., whilst he himself steps backwards with the r.f. Approaching the Master's Chair from the r.h. side the I.M. guides the W.M. to the seat as he passes the Chair himself. On reaching the Chair, I.M. instructs W.M. to drop his left hand, but retains his own in position.)

I.M. – By the G. of an Installed Master and the word …… , *(I.M. places W.M. in the Chair then drops his l.h.)* I place you in the Chair of King

Solomon according to ancient custom, feeling sure you will justify the choice the Brethren have made. *(I.M releases the G.)*.

I.M. – *(picks up Gavel)* – I now place in your hand this Gavel *(gives Gavel to W.M.)*, an emblem of power, which will enable you to keep order in the Lodge, particularly in the E. *(W.M., prompted by I.M., places Gavel on pedestal and puts on gauntlets and gloves.) (I.M. salutes W.M. with the Token of Humility*.)*

I.M. – W.M., will you now invest the I.P.M. *(D.C. comes forwards with Collar, hands it to W.M. and returns to his place.)*

W.M. – *(rises)* – W.Bro. .... , it gives me great pleasure to invest you as Immediate Past Master of the Lodge *(W.M. does so)*. It is not within anyone's authority to confer this honour upon you, it being yours of right, you having faithfully discharged your duties as Master of the Lodge. However, from the capable manner in which you have conducted the affairs of the Lodge during your Mastership, I feel sure that whenever I require assistance, your help will be readily forthcoming. *(W.M. sits)*.

I.M. – Brethren, I call upon you to salute the W.M. as I.Ms. in passing, following and copying the D.C. *(D.C., squaring the Lodge,*

**See description of Sn. (Page 25)*

proceeds to NE corner and faces S. Brethren form up suitably to follow him. D.C. and Brethren salute the W.M. as I.Ms. in passing with the penal Sn. and remain standing on the floor of the Lodge.)

I.M. – Brethren, I call upon you to greet the W.M. with 'five', taking the time from the D.C.

D.C. – Brethren, the salutation to the W.M. is the Token of Humility** five times *(all turn toward the W.M.)* To order, Brethren. *(D.C. and Brethren give the greeting together and all resume their seats.)*

If a break is desired, it should be effected by a formal Calling Off at this point. [See main Ritual Book], after which the D.C. attends to the T. B., and the I.M. closes the V.S.L.* without removing the S. and Cs., and replaces the Working Tools and returns to his place.

This is also the convenient moment when the Lodge Collars can be placed at W. of Secretary's table, adjacent to a seat to be occupied by the A.D.C. I.M. ensures that the Warrant of the Lodge and copies of the B. of C. and By-Laws are available at the W.M.'s pedestal together with the selection of booklets recommended by Grand Lodge.

* *See General Note.*

** *Alternatively the G. or R.Sn. may be given.*

On the return, the Lodge is Called On [See main Ritual Book] after which the D.C. attends to the T.B., and the I.M. reopens the V.S.L*. and ensures the S. and Cs. are still correctly positioned, displays or arranges the Working Tools and returns to his place.

IT HAS BEEN RECOMMENDED THAT WITH THE LODGE STILL FORMED AS A BOARD OF INSTALLED MASTERS, THE SIGN GIVEN BY THE J.W. IN THE CALLING OFF CEREMONY SHOULD BE THE P.Sn. OF AN I.M.

I.M. – W.M., will you now please close this Board of Installed Masters.

W.M. – Brethren, I declare this Board of Installed Masters closed. *(W.M. sounds his Gavel, one k., which is answered by S.W. and J.W. All remain seated.)*

* *See General Note.*

CEREMONY OF INSTALLATION
PART 2

The I.M. then takes position in the E at l. of W.M.'s pedestal where he remains standing until the commencement of the Investiture of Officers, except as directed by the rubric.

I.M. – Bro I.G. *(who advances on to the edge of S.P. and gives Sp. and P.Sn. of Third Degree)*, admit all M.Ms.

(I.G. drops P.Sn., goes to the door and opens it)

I.G. – *(Speaks across the threshold)* – Will all M.M.s. please enter the Lodge, visiting Brethren first.

(Meanwhile, D.C., squaring the Lodge, goes to NW corner to meet the M.Ms., who enter without saluting. D.C. selects a convenient number of M.Ms., ranges them along the N and positions himself at E end of the line, all facing S. The remainder of the M.Ms. proceed to seats in the Lodge. I.G. locks door, advances on to edge of S.P. and gives Sp. and P.Sn. of Third Degree.)

I.G. – Bro. I.M., all M.Ms. have been admitted. *(drops P.Sn. and returns to his seat)*

I.M. – Brethren, during your temporary absence

our highly esteemed Bro. *(full name)* has been duly installed in the Chair of K.S. according to ancient custom and I call upon you to salute him as M.Ms. in passing, following and copying our Brother, the D.C.

D.C. – *(to M.Ms. in line)* – L. turn Brethren.

(D.C. and M.Ms. turn l. and, squaring the Lodge, salute the W.M. as M.Ms. in passing. Returning along the N, all halt and turn to face S; D.C. leaves enough space from NE corner for any F.Cs. to join the line later.)

I.M. – Brethren, for the first time and in the E, I proclaim Bro. *(full name)* W.M. of the ....Lodge, Number .... *(worded in full)* on the Register of the Grand Lodge of England, for the ensuing twelve months and until a successor shall have been duly elected and installed in his stead and I call upon you to greet him as M.Ms. with 'three', taking the time from our Brother, the D.C.

(D.C. squaring the Lodge, places his Wand in its stand as he moves to a convenient position in the SE, turns and faces N.)

D.C. – Brethren, the salutation in this Degree is the G. or R.Sn. three times. Half l. turn Brethren. *(Brethren turn h.l.; D.C. turns h.r.)* To order Brethren. *(D.C. and Brethren give the greeting together)* Half r. turn Brethren. *(D.C. moves to SE corner and stands near his seat, facing N.)*

I.M. – W.M., I now present to your notice the working tools of a M.M., which are the Sk., the Pl., and the Cs. *(picks up each working tool in turn and shows it to the W.M.)*. You are so well acquainted with their uses that I need not here explain them at length. *(I.M. replaces working tools)* You will therefore close the Lodge in this Degree or resume it in the Second.

(The Lodge may then be closed in the Third Degree. If resumed in the Second Degree, W.M. sound his Gavel, one k, followed by S.W. and J.W.)

W.M. – Brethren, by the power in me vested, I resume the Lodge in the Second Degree. *(W.M. gives ks. of Second Degree, followed by S.W. and J.W., I.G. and Tyler. D.C. attends to T.B., returns to SE corner, and stands near his seat, facing N; I.M. comes forward to front of W.M.'s pedestal, adjusts S. and Cs. and returns to his position in the E.*

I.M. – Bro. I.G. *(who advances on to edge of S.P. and gives Sp. and Sn. of Second Degree)*, admit all F.Cs. *(I.G. cuts Sn., goes to door and opens it)*

I.G. – *(speaks across the threshold)* – Will all F.Cs. please enter the Lodge.

(F.Cs., if any, enter without saluting and are met by D.C. who escorts them to E end of line. Visiting F.Cs. may go to convenient seats. I.G. locks door,

advances on to edge of S.P. and gives Sp. and Sn. of Second Degree.)

I.G. – Bro. I.M., all F.Cs. have been admitted. *(cuts Sn. and returns to his seat)*

I.M. – Brethren, during your temporary absence our highly esteemed Bro. *(full name)* has been duly installed in the Chair of K.S. according to ancient custom and I call upon you to salute him as F.Cs. in passing, following and copying our Brother, the D.C.

D.C. – L. turn Brethren. *(D.C. and Brethren turn l. and, squaring the Lodge, salute the W.M. as F.Cs. in passing. Returning along the N, all halt and turn to face S; D.C. leaves enough space from NE corner for any E.A. to join the line later. I.M., squaring the Lodge, follows the Brethren round to l. of S.W.'s pedestal where he stands on edge of S.P., and faces E.)*

I.M. – Brethren, for the second time and in the W, I proclaim Bro. *(full name)* W.M. of the ....Lodge, Number .... *(worded in full)* on the Register of the Grand Lodge of England, for the ensuing twelve months and until a successor shall have been duly elected and installed in his stead and I call upon you to greet him as F.Cs. with 'five', taking the time from our Brother, the D.C. *(I.M. remains standing in the W.)*

(D.C. squaring the Lodge, places his Wand in its

stand as he moves to a convenient position in the SE, turns and faces N.)

D.C. – Brethren, the salutation in this Degree is b.h.b. five times to the rhythm of the F.C. knocks, thus. *(D.C. demonstrates once)* Half l. turn Brethren. *(Brethren turn h.l.; D.C. turns h.r.)* To order Brethren, as F.Cs. *(D.C. and Brethren stand to order as F.Cs. and give the greeting together)* Half r. turn Brethren. *(D.C. moves to SE corner and stands near his seat, facing N. I.M., squaring the Lodge, returns to his position in the E.)*

I.M. – W.M., I now present to your notice the working tools of a F.C.F.,which are the S., the L. and the P.R. *(picks up each working tool in turn and shows it to the W.M.)*. You are so well acquainted with their uses that I need not here explain them at length. *(I.M. replaces working tools)* You will therefore close the Lodge in this Degree or resume it in the First.

(The Lodge may then be closed in the Second Degree. If resumed in the First Degree, W.M. sound his Gavel, one k, followed by S.W. and J.W.)

W.M. – Brethren, by the power in me vested, I resume the Lodge in the First Degree. *(W.M. gives ks. of First Degree, followed by S.W. and J.W., I.G. and Tyler. D.C. attends to T.B., returns to SE corner, and stands near his seat, facing N; I.M. comes forward to front of W.M.'s pedestal,* *adjusts S. and Cs. and returns to his position in the E.)*

I.M. – Bro. I.G. *(who advances on to edge of S.P. and gives Sp. and Sn. of First Degree)*, admit all E.As. *(I.G. cuts Sn., goes to door and opens it)*

I.G. – *(speaks across the threshold)* – Will all E.As. please enter the Lodge.

(E.As., if any, enter without saluting and are met by D.C. who escorts them to E end of line. Visiting E.As. may go to convenient seats. I.G. locks door, advances on to edge of S.P. and gives Sp. and Sn. of First Degree.)

I.G. – Bro. I.M., all E.As. have been admitted. *(cuts Sn. and returns to his seat)*

I.M. – Brethren, during your temporary absence our highly esteemed Bro. *(full name)* has been duly installed in the Chair of K.S. according to ancient custom and I call upon you to salute him as E.As. in passing, following and copying our Brother, the D.C.

D.C. – L. turn Brethren. *(D.C. and Brethren turn l. and, squaring the Lodge, salute the W.M. as E.As. in passing. Returning along the N, all halt and turn to face S; I.M., follows the Brethren as far as the l. of J.W.'s pedestal where he stands on edge of S.P., and faces N.)*

I.M. – Brethren, for the third time and in the S, I proclaim Bro. *(full name)* W.M. of the ……….Lodge, Number ………. *(worded in full)* on the Register of the Grand Lodge of England, for the ensuing twelve months and until a successor shall have been duly elected and installed in his stead and I call upon you to greet him as E.As. with 'three', taking the time from our Brother, the D.C. *(I.M. remains standing in the S.)*

(D.C. squaring the Lodge, places his Wand in its stand as he moves to a convenient position in the SE, turns and faces N.)

D.C. – Brethren, the salutation in this Degree is the E.A. Sn. three times. Half l. turn Brethren. *(Brethren turn h.l.; D.C. turns h.r.)* To order Brethren. *(D.C. and Brethren give the greeting together)* Half r. turn Brethren. *(D.C. moves to SE corner and stands near his seat, facing N. I.M., squaring the Lodge at Secretary's table, returns to his position in the E.)*

I.M. – W.M., I now present to your notice the working tools of an E.A.F., which are the 24-inch G., the C.G. and the C. *(picks up each working tool in turn and shows it to the W.M.)*. You are so well acquainted with their uses that I need not here explain them at length. *(I.M. replaces working tools)*

I.M. – W.M. *(who rises)*, I now deliver into your keeping the Warrant of the Lodge. *(I.M. opens the Warrant, shows it to W.M., folds it and replaces it in its case)* It has for many years been entrusted to the care of worthy and distinguished Brethren and

I am sure that whilst it is in your charge it will lose none of its lustre, but will be transmitted to your successor, pure and unsullied, as you now receive it. *(I.M. hands Warrant to W.M.)* I also present to you the Book of Constitutions *(hands B of C to W.M.)*,which I strongly commend to your serious perusal, for you will find there is scarcely a case of difficulty can occur in the Lodge which a reference to that book *(points to B of C)* will not set right; likewise the By-Laws of the Lodge *(hands By-Laws to W.M.)*, together with certain booklets highly commended by Grand Lodge, for your information. *(W.M. sits and places Warrant, B of C, and By-Laws on pedestal shelf)*

I.M. – Brethren be seated. *(Brethren standing in the N turn left and, squaring the Lodge, proceed to their seats. D.C. sits.)*

(The Hall Stone Jewel should be presented at this point.)

I.M. – W.M., will you now please appoint and invest your officers. *(I.M. gives Sp. and Sn. of First Degree, and sits.)*

END OF THE CEREMONY OF INSTALLATION

INDUCTION OF A PAST MASTER

(The Lodge being open in the First Degree, the W.M. sounds his gavel, one k., which is answered by the S.W. and J.W.)

W.M. – W.Bro. *(surname only, who rises and gives Sp. and Sn. of First Degree)* will you please occupy the S.W.'s chair. *(W.Bro. cuts Sn.)*

(D.C., squaring the Lodge, conducts the W.Bro. to r. of S.W. who removes his gauntlets and leaves them on top of the pedestal to await the newly invested S.W. Retaining his collar of office, S.W. vacates chair in favour of the W.Bro., who salutes W.M. in the First Degree and sits. D.C., squaring the Lodge, conducts the retiring S.W. to a seat in the NE and returns to his own seat.)

W.M. – *(sounds his Gavel, one k., which is answered by S.W. and J.W.)* – W.Bro. *(surname only, who rises and gives Sp. and Sn. of First Degree)*, will you please occupy the J.W.'s chair. *(W.Bro. cuts Sn.)*

(D.C., squaring the Lodge, conducts the W.Bro. to r. of J.W. who removes his gauntlets and leaves them on top of the pedestal to await the newly invested J.W. Retaining his collar of office, J.W.

vacates chair in favour of the W.Bro. who salutes W.M. in the First Degree and sits. D.C., squaring the Lodge, conducts the retiring J.W. to a seat in the NE and returns to his own seat.)

W.M. – *(sounds his Gavel, one k., which is answered by S.W. and J.W.)* – W.Bro. *(surname only, who rises and gives Sp. and Sn. of First Degree)*, will you please act as I.G. *(W.Bro. cuts Sn.)*

(D.C., squaring the Lodge, conducts the W.Bro. to the I.G. Retaining his collar of office, I.G. vacates his seat in favour of the W.Bro., who salutes W.M. in the First Degree and sits. D.C., squaring the Lodge, conducts the retiring I.G. to a seat in the NE and returns to his own seat.)

W.M. – *(sounds his Gavel, one k., which is answered by S.W. and J.W.)* – Bro. Chaplain, Bro. Secretary, Bro.D.C., Bro.A.D.C. and Bro. Organist *(who all rise and give Sp. and Sn. of First Degree)*, will you please continue to act in your respective offices. *(the five officers cut Sn. and sit)*

W.M. – *(sounds his Gavel, one k., which is answered by S.W. and J.W.)* – Brethren, I now request the officers of my year to assemble in line along the N.

(The officers, squaring the Lodge where necessary, line-up under D.C.'s guidance along the N, and face S; the W.M. here usually addresses

them with a general expression of thanks for their services during the year.)

W.M. – Will you now please file past so that I can thank you individually and will you then please return the collar with which I had the pleasure of investing you, to our Brother, the I.P.M., in passing.

(The officers turn left and, squaring the Lodge at NE corner, file past W.M. who rises, personally greets each officer in turn at l. of pedestal, and resumes his seat. Meanwhile, the I.P.M. has taken up a suitable position in SE. The officers, as they pass the I.P.M. remove their collars of office and hand them to him. Squaring the Lodge where necessary, the Chaplain, Secretary, D.C., A.D.C. and the Organist return to their usual places, while the remainder of the officers proceed to vacant seats in the Lodge. I.P.M. transfers collars to A.D.C. The Lodge is then opened in the Second Degree; D.C. attends to T.B. M.E., who is seated in the NE, removes his gloves and rises. D.C., squaring the Lodge, conducts the M.E. to a suitable position in mid-line of the Lodge, and stands to his r., both facing W.M.

D.C.- *(gives Sp. and Sn. of Second Degree)*- W.M., I present to you W.Bro. *(full name)* Master Elect of this Lodge, to receive at your hands the benefit of Installation.

W.M.- Bro. D.C., your presentation shall be attended to, but I must first address a few observations to the Brethren. *(D.C. cuts Sn. and squaring the Lodge, returns to his seat; M.E. remains standing facing W.M.)*

W.M.- *(sounds his Gavel one k, which is answered by S.W. and J.W.)* – Brethren, from time immemorial it has been an established custom among Freemasons for each Lodge, once in every year at a stated period, to select from its Wardens and past Wardens a skilled Craftsman to preside over them in the capacity of Master. He must have been regularly balloted for and elected by the Master, Wardens and Brethren in open Lodge assembled and be presented to a Board of Installed Masters to receive from a predecessor the benefit of Installation, the better to qualify him for the duties of that important trust. W.Bro. *(Surname only)* you having been so elected, and having been installed on a previous occasion, I must ask if you re-affirm your promise to submit to and support the Charges and Regulations then read to you.

M.E.- I do.

W.M.- Then you will please step this way and recite the S.O. of Master Elect. You will kneel as a F.C. (*or*, – *You will be covered.) *(this done, M.E. places his r.h. on the V.S.L. and shows H.Sn. W.M. sounds his gavel one k., which is answered by S.W.*

**Alternative wording should the Cand. be Jewish*

and J.W. All rise and without taking Sp., come to order with Sn. of F.)

OBLIGATION

W.M.- State your names at length and recite your Obligation.

M.E.- *I* (*states his full name*) in the presence of T.G.G.O.T.U. and of this worthy and worshipful Lodge of F.C.Fs., regularly held, assembled and properly dedicated, do agree to accept the office of Master of this Lodge; and the duties of that high station, zealously, faithfully, and impartially to administer, to the best of my skill and ability, until the next period of election within the Lodge and until a successor shall have been duly elected and installed in my stead. I further solemnly promise that I will not, either during my Mastership, or at any time the Lodge may be under my direction, permit or suffer any deviation from the Ancient Customs and established Landmarks of the Order. I will not administer, nor suffer to be administered, any rite or ceremony contrary to, or subversive of, our Ancient Institution, but will maintain and uphold, pure and unsullied, the genuine principles and tenets of the Craft. I will observe, and to the utmost of my power enforce, a due obedience to those Charges and Regulations to which I have already given my assent, and in every respect conscientiously discharge my duties as a Ruler in the Craft and Master of this Lodge. So help me A.G. and keep me steadfast in this the S.O. of Master Elect.

(M.E. drops H. Sn.)

W.M. – As a pledge of fidelity and to render what you have repeated a S.O. you will salute the V. of the S.L.t. *(M.E. does so; all drop Sn. of F.; W.M. takes M.E.'s r.h. in his own)*. Rise, (*or*, *Be uncovered,) duly obligated, Master Elect.

(W.M. sits and Brethren resume their seats. D.C., squaring the Lodge, conducts M.E. to a seat in the SE and returns to his own seat. The Lodge is then opened in the Third Degree; D.C. attends to T.B.)

W.M.- *(sounds his Gavel one k., which is answered by S.W. and J.W.)* – Brethren, I must now request all below the rank of Installed Master to retire from the Lodge. *(I.G. goes to the door, opens it, and retiring Brethren leave the Lodge without saluting: I.G. locks door and returns to his seat.)*

**Alternative wording if the Cand. be Jewish*

INNER WORKING

(The Brethren below the rank of Installed Master having retired from the Lodge, the A.D.C., squaring the Lodge, places kneeling stool in the centre of the Lodge and returns to his seat. D.C.,

squaring the Lodge, conducts M.E. to kneeling stool and both stand facing E. I.M. sounds his gavel, one k., which is answered by S.W. and J.W.)

I.M. – Brethren, I declare this a duly constituted Board of Installed Masters.

D.C. – *(gives P.Sn. of an I.M.)* – W.M., I present to this Board of Installed Masters, W.Bro............. *(M.E.'s full name)*, duly obligated M.E., to receive from your hands the benefit of Installation.

I.M. – Bro. D.C., your presentation shall be attended to. *(D.C. drops P.Sn. and returns to his seat: M.E. remains standing.)*

I.M. – *(sounds his Gavel, one k., which is answered by S.W. and J.W.)* Bro. – *(M.E.'s name)* – You will kneel on both knees. *(or,* – *You will be covered.) Brethren, let us pray. *(Brethren rise, turn to face E., give Sn. of R. and may kneel on one k. on a convenient seat.)*

Chaplain or I.M. – Vouchsafe Thine aid Almighty Father, Supreme Governor of the Universe, to our solemn rite and grant that this worthy and distinguished Brother, who is again to be numbered among the rulers in the Craft, may be endued with wisdom to comprehend, judgment to define, and ability to enforce obedience to Thy Divine laws. Sanctify him by Thy grace, strengthen him with Thy power, and enrich his

**Alternative wording if the Cand. be Jewish*

mind with genuine knowledge, that he may be the better enabled to enlighten the minds of the Brethren and to consecrate this our mansion to the honour and glory of Thy Most Holy Name.

ALL – *(the following response may be chanted)* – So mote it be. *(all drop Sn. of R. Brethren resume standing position; M.E. rises, or, if Jewish, remains covered until after his affirmation. A.D.C., squaring the Lodge, removes kneeling stool and returns to his place.)*

I.M. – *(to M.E.)* Bro.......... *(Surname only)*, you have already taken an Obligation as regards your duties as Master of the Lodge. Do you now re-affirm the Obligation you took as an Installed Master, to preserve inviolate the secrets restricted to the Master's Chair?

M.E.- I do. *(M.E., if Jewish, is uncovered).*

I.M.- You will please step this way, place your r.h. on the V.S.L., and remain standing. *(M.E. does so.)*

I.M. – Let me once more direct your attention to the three G.Ls. in Freemasonry, which are the V. of the S.L., the S. and the Cs. *(I.M. points to each in turn)*. The V. of the S.L. is that G.L. which will guide you to all truth, direct your steps in the paths of happiness and point out to you the whole duty of man. The S. teaches you to regulate your life and actions according to Masonic line and rule and to harmonise your conduct by the principles of morality and virtue. The Cs. remind you to limit your desires in every station of life, so that, rising to eminence by merit, you may live respected and die regretted. *(I.M. removes gauntlets, places them on pedestal and moves out of the pedestal to r. of M.E and moves him clockwise away from the pedestal and places him in the SE facing N; steps back three paces and stands facing him; all remain standing.)*

I.M.- The Traditional History was explained to you on a former occasion. Likewise you are already in possession of the secrets of an Installed Master and you wear the badge of that rank. I shall therefore invest you with the Master's Collar *(I.M. removes his Collar of Office and invests M.E. as W.M.)*, which is the highest honour the Lodge can confer on any of its members. To this Collar is attached the S. *(I.M. indicates the Jewel)*, an instrument which forms the rude and proves the perfect mass and is justly applied by Installed Masters to inculcate the principles of piety and virtue. Masonically speaking it should be the guide of all your actions.

(I.M., with his r.h., grips the W.M. with the G. of an Installed Master, places on his own l.s. the l.h. of the W.M. and places his own l.h. on the l.s. of the W.M. Maintaining the relative positions of the a. and h., I.M. instructs the W.M. to step off with the l.f., whilst he himself steps backwards with the r.f. Approaching the Master's Chair from the r.h. side

the I.M. guides the W.M. to the seat as he passes the Chair himself. On reaching the Chair, I.M. instructs W.M. to drop his left hand, but retains his own in position.)

I.M. – By the G. of an Installed Master and the word ...... , *(I.M. places W.M. in the Chair then drops his l.h.)* I place you in the Chair of King Solomon according to ancient custom, feeling sure you will justify the choice the Brethren have made. *(I.M releases the G.)*.

I.M. – *(picks up Gavel)* – I now place in your hand this Gavel *(gives Gavel to W.M.)*, an emblem of power, which will enable you to keep order in the Lodge, particularly in the E. *(W.M., prompted by I.M., places Gavel on pedestal and puts on gauntlets and gloves.) (I.M. salutes W.M. with the Token of Humility.) {This salute could be construed as being similar to a Cavalier doffing his hat.}*

I.M. – W.M., will you now invest the I.P.M. *(D.C. comes forwards with Collar, hands it to W.M. and returns to his place.)*

W.M. – *(rises)* – W.Bro. .... , it gives me great pleasure to invest you as Immediate Past Master of the Lodge *(W.M. does so)*. It is not within anyone's authority to confer this honour upon you, it being yours of right, you having faithfully discharged your duties as Master of the Lodge. However, from the capable manner in which you have conducted the affairs of the Lodge during your Mastership, I feel sure that whenever I require assistance, your help will be readily forthcoming. *(W.M. sits)*

I.M. – Brethren, I call upon you to salute the W.M. as I.Ms. in passing, following and copying the D.C. *(D.C., squaring the Lodge, proceeds to NE corner and faces S. Brethren form up suitably and follow him. D.C. and Brethren salute the W.M. as I.Ms. in passing with the penal Sn. and remain standing on the floor of the Lodge.)*

I.M. – Brethren, I call upon you to greet the W.M. with 'five', taking the time from the D.C.

D.C. – Brethren, the salutation to the W.M. is the Token of Humility* five times *(all turn toward the W.M.)* To order, Brethren. *(D.C. and Brethren give the greeting together and all resume their seats)*

I.M. – W.M., will you now please close this Board of Installed Masters.

W.M. – Brethren, I declare this Board of Installed Masters closed. *(W.M. sounds his Gavel, one k., which is answered by S.W. and J.W. All remain seated.)*

**Alternatively the G. or R.Sn. sign may be given.*

CEREMONY OF INSTALLATION

PART 2 (See page 30)

MASTER CONTINUING IN OFFICE FOR SECOND YEAR

The Master having been elected to serve for a further successive year (by Dispensation if more than two), the item on the summons should read "To proclaim W.Bro. (full name) as Master."

(The Lodge being open in the First Degree, the W.M. sounds his Gavel, one k., which is answered by S.W. and J.W.)

W.M. – W. Bro. *(surname only, who rises and gives Sp. and Sn. of First Degree)*, will you please occupy the S.W.'s chair. *(W.Bro. cuts Sn.)*

(D.C., squaring the Lodge, conducts the W.Bro. to r. of S.W. who removes his gauntlets and leaves them on top of the pedestal to await the newly invested S.W. Retaining his collar of office, S.W. vacates chair in favour of the W.Bro., who salutes W.M. in the First Degree and sits. D.C., squaring the Lodge, conducts the retiring S.W. to a seat in the NE and returns to his own seat.)

W.M. – *(sounds his Gavel, one k., which is answered by S.W. and J.W.)* – W.Bro. *(surname only, who rises and gives Sp. and Sn. of First Degree)*, will you please occupy the J.W.'s chair. *(W.Bro. cuts Sn.)*

(D.C., squaring the Lodge, conducts the W.Bro. to r. of J.W. who removes his gauntlets and leaves them on top of the pedestal to await the newly invested J.W. Retaining his collar of office, J.W. vacates chair in favour of the W.Bro. who salutes W.M. in the First Degree and sits. D.C., squaring the Lodge, conducts the retiring J.W. to a seat in the NE and returns to his own seat.)

W.M. – *(sounds his Gavel, one k., which is answered by S.W. and J.W.)* – W.Bro. *(surname only, who rises and gives Sp. and Sn. of First Degree)*, will you please act as I.G. *(W.Bro. cuts Sn.)*

(D.C., squaring the Lodge, conducts the W.Bro. to the I.G. Retaining his collar of office, I.G. vacates his seat in favour of the W.Bro., who salutes W.M. in the First Degree and sits. D.C., squaring the Lodge, conducts the retiring I.G. to a seat in the NE and returns to his own seat.)

W.M. – *(sounds his Gavel, one k., which is answered by S.W. and J.W.)* – Bro. Chaplain, Bro. Secretary, Bro.D.C., Bro.A.D.C. and Bro. Organist *(who all rise and give Sp. and Sn. of First Degree)*, will you please continue to act in your respective offices. *(the five officers cut Sn. and sit)*

W.M. – *(sounds his Gavel, one k., which is answered by S.W. and J.W.)* – Brethren, I now request the officers of my year to assemble in line along the N.

(The officers, squaring the Lodge where necessary, line-up under D.C.'s guidance along the N, and face S; the W.M. here usually addresses them with a general expression of thanks for their services during the year.)

W.M. – Will you now please file past so that I can thank you individually and will you then please return the collar with which I had the pleasure of investing you, to our Brother, the I.P.M., in passing.

(The officers turn left and, squaring the Lodge at NE corner, file past W.M. who rises, personally greets each officer in turn at l. of pedestal, and resumes his seat. Meanwhile, the I.P.M. has taken up a suitable position in SE. The officers, as they pass the I.P.M. remove their collars of office and hand them to him. Squaring the Lodge where necessary, the Chaplain, Secretary, D.C., A.D.C. and the Organist return to their usual places, while the remainder of the officers proceed to vacant seats in the Lodge. I.P.M. transfers collars to A.D.C.

D.C. or I.P.M. – *(from SE)*- Brethren, I proclaim W.Bro. *(full name)* Worshipful Master of this the ....Lodge, Number........... on the Register of the Grand Lodge of England, for the ensuing twelve months and until a successor shall have been duly elected and installed in his stead. I now ask you all to rise *(Brethren all stand)* and I call upon you to greet him as E.As with 'three'.

The salutation is the E.A. Sn. three times. Turn towards the W.M. To order Brethren. *(D.C. and Brethren give the greeting together.)*

I.P.M. or I.M. – Brethren be seated.

For continuation of the Ceremony —— see the General Notes page 11.

ISBN 978-0-85318-249-8